# THE COMPLETE POTTER:

# THROWING

*Porcelain bowl by Lucie Rie.*

# THE COMPLETE POTTER:
# THROWING

RICHARD PHETHEAN

SERIES EDITOR EMMANUEL COOPER

B. T. Batsford Ltd, London

First published 1993

British Library Cataloguing-in-Publication
Data.
A catalogue record for this book is available
from the British Library.

ISBN 0 7134 6648 0

Typeset by Servis Filmsetting Ltd
and printed in Hong Kong
for the publishers
B. T. Batsford Ltd
4 Fitzhardinge Street
London W1H OAH

**Front cover**
*The author at the wheel,*
*refining the pouring lip on a jug.*

**Back cover**
*Lidded jar by the author.*
*Flanged lid with pulled handle.*
*Slip-decorated earthenware,*
*35 cm high.*

## DEDICATION

For Jean and Tom

## ACKNOWLEDGEMENTS

To David Henderson for his advice, time and
care in mounting the sequence photography.

To Colin Pearson and Janice Tchalenko for
their guidance, support and encouragement
over the years.

A video cassette *Introduction to Throwing*
is available from:
Richard Phethean
23, Rollscourt Avenue
London SE24 0EA
Please write for information, including a
stamped addressed envelope.

# CONTENTS

# INTRODUCTION

Throwing is the action of forming an amorphous mass of clay into shapes with circular symmetry, using a revolving flat turntable or potter's wheel. To watch a skilled potter effortlessly transforming this soft, lifeless material into something of enduring form, character and vitality 'before your very eyes' has a captivating magic. Made to look so inviting, it can grip you with an overwhelming desire to have a go. However, faced with a spinning ball of clay, the beginner often finds the procedure shrouded in impenetrable mystery.

Learning to throw is like learning to play a musical instrument. Basic principles must be absorbed and techniques must be practised many times before tangible progress is achieved. Throwing is only a part of the more complete process involved in making finished pottery vessels. This book looks at the whole process, which can be broadly divided into four categories:

1 *preparation* – of equipment and materials
2 *throwing* – wheelwork with wet or 'plastic' clay
3 *turning* – wheelwork with semi-dry or 'leather-hard' clay
4 *detailing* – functional and ornamental refinements

My aim is first to break down the apparently seamless, organic nature of throwing into the basic techniques, and to examine their significance in the growth of a pot. Then, since many thrown forms evolve from a common root, the study of common vessel types focuses on the later stages of refinement and their specialized functions. Lastly, ways to decorate and distort thrown clay forms are discussed and illustrated with examples of finished work.

The history of vessel-making in this manner is as ancient as civilization itself. Many classic periods, in pottery terms, produced wares of such outstanding simple beauty that they continue to inspire new devotees to the craft.

Today the approaches to throwing are as varied as in any field of the arts and crafts. The spectrum spans a diverse use of clays, glazes and firing techniques, from the delicate translucency of porcelain to the robust earthiness of terracotta, from vibrant primary colour to subtle natural hues, and from the familiar homeliness of domestic ware to the dramatic impact of sculpture. All these qualities are expressible in this medium.

This book does not try to view throwing from a particular standpoint. It simply aims to analyse the strengths and weaknesses of thrown forms and vessel function, enabling readers to pursue their own avenues of interest better equipped to identify and overcome particular problems.

*(Right) Earthenware jar by Michael Cardew. Photo courtesy of* Ceramic Review.

*(Far right) Form assembled from thrown elements by Hans Coper. Photo courtesy of* Ceramic Review.

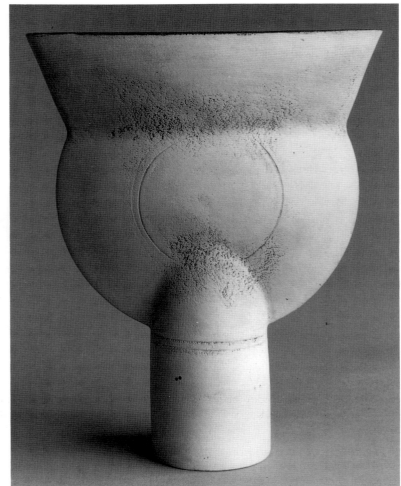

# CHAPTER ONE

# EQUIPMENT AND MATERIALS

## THE POTTER'S WHEEL

Historically, the potter's wheel was the simplest of machines. It consisted of a flat turntable of wood or stone centred on a pivot, whose weight provided the momentum to keep it revolving so that the clay could be worked in the potter's hands. Modern studio wheels still use exactly the same principle, merely incorporating devices that increase the potter's comfort, make the wheels more efficient and easier to control, and decrease the amount of physical labour required.

Treadle and gearing systems have been added to kick wheels, and tough motors with a variety of drive transmissions to power wheels. All have slip trays to keep the potter clean and dry, and wheelheads which can be detached and replaced with another, for more specialized use. Electric wheels typically have top speeds of 200–300 r p m, but high speed in itself is much less important than torque (the ability to maintain a constant speed against the pressure of the hands on the clay and wheelhead) and control at very slow speeds.

A good throwing position, whether seated

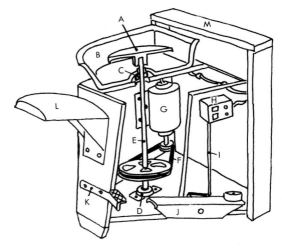

A: wheelhead
B: slip tray
C: top bearing
D: bottom bearing
E: drive-shaft
F: drive belt
G: motor

H: rheostat – on/off switch
I: foot pedal/rheostat linkage
J: foot pedal
K: foot rest
L: seat
M: pot shelf

or standing, is important. The upper half of the body needs to be able to lean over the wheelhead to give support to your hands and arms. A wheel with a built-in seat can usually be adjusted if necessary. For wheels without a seat, either choose a stool or chair that gives you a comfortable height at which to work, or put the wheel on a plinth or bench at a suitable height if you prefer to stand. With stand-up wheels, you may need to use a low step to raise yourself to the ideal height.

The diagram on the left shows the workings of a modern electric wheel. The foot pedal is connected to a rheostat, which varies the current to the motor to control its speed. Here the drive is connected to the drive-shaft via a belt similar to the fanbelt in a car. The drive-shaft spins freely on two bearings. The top one, housed in a protective bulge in the slip tray, is always the part that is most vulnerable to damage, so care should be taken *never* to allow the tray to overfill with water and slurry.

*(Above left) A modern electric potter's wheel.*

*Throwing position.*

## TOOLS

A potter's tool kit is usually a mixture of bought, improvised and hand-made implements which over a period of time builds into a very personal collection.

Not everything you need to buy has to come from a specialist pottery supplier. Hardware and DIY shops are a good source of effective and cheaper alternatives. Some of your most treasured and valuable tools may come from the kitchen drawer or from household odds and ends of wood, metal or plastic.

### FOR THROWING BEGINNERS

There are a few essentials which every 'starter pack' should contain, but as you progress to making a wider range of forms and vessels, your tool box will have to carry an assortment of cutting, scraping, scratching and measuring implements as well. A typical selection is illustrated overleaf. Where more than one item is shown, any one will do.

### PROTECTIVE CLOTHING

Whatever type of apron or overalls you choose to wear, short-sleeved or sleeveless ones are desirable to keep your hands and arms unhindered at all times. A nylon all-in-one suit will protect you most effectively from water and heavy soiling. Nylon is easily washed, and retains less dust than cotton. Keep a fresh towel within reach or on your lap as you begin each session on the wheel.

## CLAYS

Plasticity is the term used for the unique property which clay has of being readily moulded into shape.

When the smooth, flat, microscopic particles of clay are mixed with water, the water's surface tension acts like magnetism, allowing the particles to slide across each other while resisting separation. As the water evaporates, the clay shrinks and the particles knit together, retaining the shape made in rigid form.

The purer, whiter 'primary' clays (i.e. clays found in their site of origin) have large, coarse particles. The darker 'secondary' clays (i.e. clays weathered from their original site, mixed with other elements and laid down in sedimentary beds elsewhere) have smaller, smoother particles (because they have been worn in the same way that jagged rocks falling from a sea cliff are eventually worn by the waves into smooth pebbles), and subsequently become much more plastic.

A throwing clay has to have good plasticity, but in order to fulfil a potter's needs of temperature, colour, texture and strength, recipes of clays and other materials are blended into clay 'bodies'.

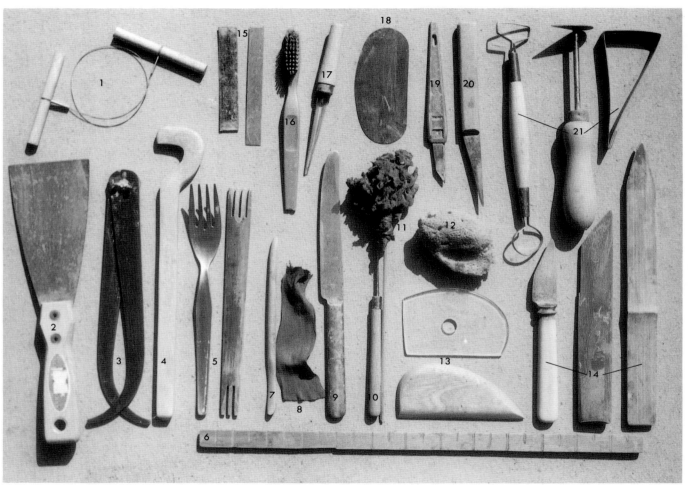

*A range of potter's tools.*

*(See left)*

### For clay preparation
1 *Cheese wire (thick wire for wedging)
2 *Bench scraper

### For throwing (wet-clay work)
*(bottom row, left to right)*
3 Callipers
4 Bellying rib
5 Combing tools
6 Shrinkage ruler
7 Modelling stick
8 *Chamois leather strip
9 Table knife
10 *Needle
11 *Natural sponge (fixed to a stick)
12 *Natural sponge
13 *Throwing ribs
14 *Bevelling tools

### For finishing (leather-hard work)
*(top row, left to right)*
15 Steel banding strips
16 Toothbrush
17 Hole borer
18 *Metal kidney
19 Craft knife
20 Piercing knife
21 *Turning tools

*Items recommended for a 'starter pack'

How and when these tools are used is explained in the text as they arise.

For example, the addition of 8–10% fine sand or grog of 40–90 mesh (fired clay which has been ground to a dust) as a 'filler' will reduce plasticity slightly, but greatly increase wet strength (the ability of clay to stand up in a tall thin wall during throwing), crack resistance (by making the material less dense, reducing thermal expansion) and warping.

Students of throwing may find it easier to use a plastic clay like red earthenware than to use a less plastic white clay like porcelain, but as their skill and experience increases, will find they are able to handle all types with confidence.

Choose a body to suit the kind of work you wish to make. Use a smooth clay for small or delicate ware, a medium-textured clay for general tableware, larger pots and ovenware, and a coarse clay for large garden pots and raku work.

## CLAY PREPARATION
Preparing your clay well and having it at the right consistency is the first essential part of successful throwing. This is very often the cause of difficulties which students might put down to their own poor techniques, undermining their confidence.

The action of centring, hollowing and thinning the clay depends heavily on how uniformly it responds to your hands, and to create a homogeneous and air-pocket-free mass, it must first be methodically wedged or kneaded. Even a fresh bag of clay, which may appear to the eye to be well mixed, could be hopelessly uneven for throwing. Manufacturers of clay bodies are unable to satisfy the needs of all potters, so what for some may be too soft, for others may be too hard. Broadly, throwing clay needs to be softer than that used for other studio techniques, but within the range of throwing techniques, some activities will require stiffer clay than others. To make the clay stand up in a tall thin wall, use a stiffer, drier mix; to make wide flat shapes, use a softer, wetter mix.

However, as you progress to using larger amounts of clay per pot, centring clay which is stiff becomes an increasingly arduous chore – a balance must be struck and ultimately only experience and personal preference will guide you.

**Preparation bench:** This should be a sturdy bench with a slightly absorbent surface such as slate or concrete, ideally fixed securely to a wall and standing on a solid floor. It should be at a height that is comfortable when lifting the clay, at about hip level. Stand on a plinth to raise yourself up if necessary.

## Wedging

This method is ideal when blending soft and hard clays, or two different clays, or mixing recycled clay with fresh.

Take roughly equal masses of clay, form them into oblong blocks and with a cutting-wire slice them together in alternate layers. Alternatively, with a bench scraper, 'butter' each hard slice with a layer of soft, sticky clay.

*Note* To show the layers clearly, in the photographs here the side of the block facing the camera has been sliced off.

*1 The oblong block is cut in half.*
*2 The front half is flipped over, lifted up and brought down with a slight forward tilt on the rear half with the layers still horizontal to the bench.*
*3 Apply just enough force to flatten the block.*
*4 Roll the clay towards you.*
*5 Lift and drop it onto its back to regain an oblong shape.*
*6 Roll the clay towards you again, lift and turn the block lengthways.*
*7 Drop the 'nose' down and hold the 'tail' up to allow the wire underneath about halfway.*
*8 Before cutting again, smooth the top surface by pushing your palm away from you (this eliminates potential air pockets).*

Providing you are careful to keep the layers on the same horizontal plane, they will double and redouble and very quickly become an indivisible, even mass.

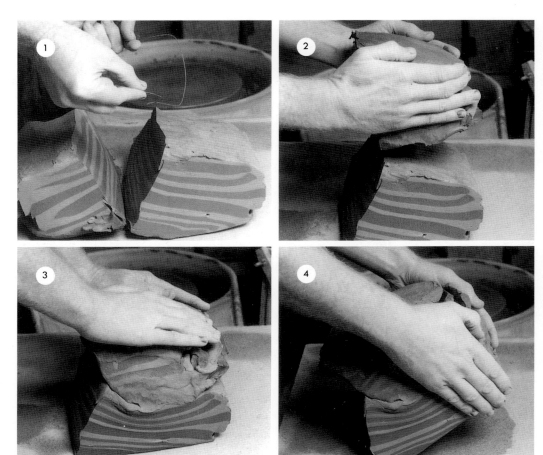

Wedging.

To check your progress, cut a 5cm thick slice out of the block. Stretching one surface into a curve will reveal air pockets, and dropping it on its edge will reveal soft and hard ridges.

As soon as your clay is ready, store in airtight conditions.

**Tips**
● Use your palms not your fingertips to grip the clay – fingertips create efficient air pockets – and take a step backwards with one foot, using your body weight to jerk the clay off the bench.
● Prepare as much clay as you can handle comfortably.
● Keep the bench scraped clean and move to a dry spot if the clay is sticking too much.
● The weight and condition of the clay will determine how much force you need to recreate the oblong shape.
● Bring the clay down with a slight tilt and thud, not a flat slap. This ensures the air is expelled and not trapped.

**Kneading**
This method is known variously as spiral, shell or bull's nose kneading, after the shapes created. The method restricts you to preparing smaller amounts of clay at a time.

It is a difficult method to describe, and students may be more successful at filling the clay with air rather than expelling it, but it is an essential technique to learn.

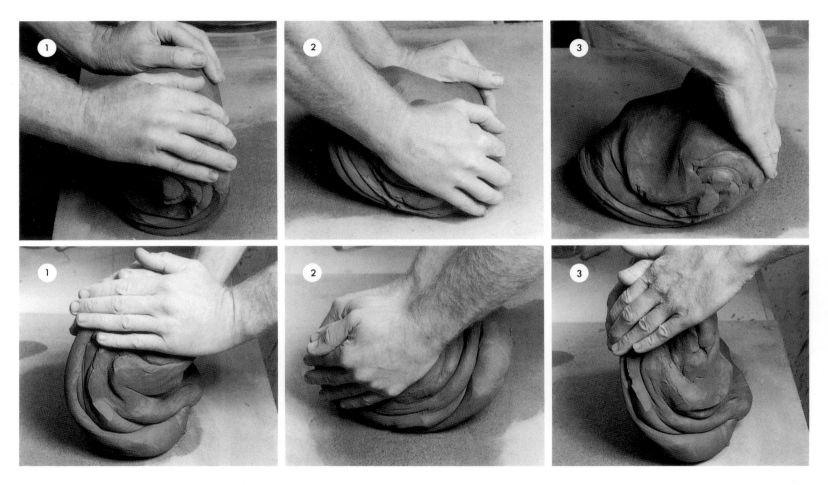

*Kneading. (Top row) Bull's nose method (Bottom row) Shell or spiral.*

### Bull's nose method (see left, top row)

*1 Push the palms down and through the clay at a 45° angle away from you.*
*2 Allow the clay to 'rock' forward.*
*3 Extend the fingers forward and 'roll' the clay back up into a 'breaking wave' shape. 'Walk' the palms forward and begin again. After several 'rock-and-rolls', roll up the clay backwards. Begin again with the roll on end.*

## Tips

● The commonest fault is to press down too hard, creating deep hollows with the palms which when rolled back enclose great pockets of air.
● If the clay wants to travel away from or towards you, keep lifting and replacing it on the centre of the bench.
● Keep patting the sides in to prevent the 'roll' width from elongating.

### Shell or spiral method (see left, bottom row)

This is essentially the same process. However, here you press forward with only one hand and the clay revolves in a circular motion creating a spiral or shell shape.

You may wish to push with either hand. Here it is the left, causing a clockwise rotation.

*1  Up in the 'breaking wave' position.*
*2  Push down and through the clay, allowing it to rock to the right.*
*3  Extend the fingers forward and roll the clay back up. Walk the palm forward and begin again.*

*Pitcher by Jim Malone. Reduced stoneware, granite and ash glaze, 35 cm high.*

# CHAPTER TWO

# FUNDAMENTAL TECHNIQUES

## CENTRING THE CLAY

Centring the clay is fundamental to successful throwing. This is the term for forming the rough ball into a smooth, flat dome which appears quite still and without the slightest oscillation, as the wheel spins. The clay then sits perfectly in the centre on the wheelhead. The condition of the clay, the position of your body, and the condition and speed of the wheel are all important in achieving this foundation stone of throwing.

Your clay pieces should be patted into rough balls (between 300 and 500 grams for beginners). To make it stick firmly, the clay is slapped on the wheel. Do this as centrally as you can. It can be pushed to a more central position before the wheel starts if you wish.

### SPEED

Electric wheels will spin at top speeds of 250–300 r p m, but beginners may find the process intimidating at such high speeds. Mild oscillations can be rapidly amplified by the centrifugal force. Potters who use kick wheels work at a fraction of this speed perfectly well,

and a slower pace can ultimately give your work more subtlety and personality. The throwing process decelerates after centring, so try beginning at perhaps 100–150 r p m or half speed.

Take up a comfortable, relaxed position that will dominate the clay. Lean against and over the wheel, using the upper-body weight to back up the power in your arms, wrists and hands. Brace your forearms by resting them on the rim of the slip-tray at about 90° to each other.

*1 All throwing techniques depend on firm control in the hands. Regard them as two halves of one tool, always working in unison and often physically linked. Everyone's hands have a left or right dominance, so to specify the left or right hand in throwing instructions may confuse or feel unnatural. You may wish to reverse the wheel's direction. Regard one hand as the 'mould' cupped around the clay, whilst the fingers of the other hand grip and brace the 'mould', pulling in the base of the palm and pressing the clay into it like a ram. Keep your hands and clay lubricated (sponge on the water, don't pour it).*

*2 Squeeze and lift the clay up into a column or cone.*

*3 Using a similar hand mould on the top and side, press the cone back down, taking care not to allow the edge to 'mushroom' over. The coning up-and-down action helps to align the clay's flat, platelet particles in circular strands and to correct any minor inconsistencies – regard it as the final fine tuning of the kneading process.*

## PROBLEMS

● *The clay hasn't stuck firmly to the wheel.* Either the wheelhead or the clay ball was coated in surface water or slurry.

● *The clay twists or tears away from the wheel in your hands.* You are using insufficient lubrication, or not lubricating often enough.

● *The clay appears to be still, and centred in your hands, but when you release it, there is a wobble.* Clay is slightly elastic, and when you grip it, you are unconsciously pulling or pushing it off its central axis. If you release your grip with a sudden jerk, like a rubber

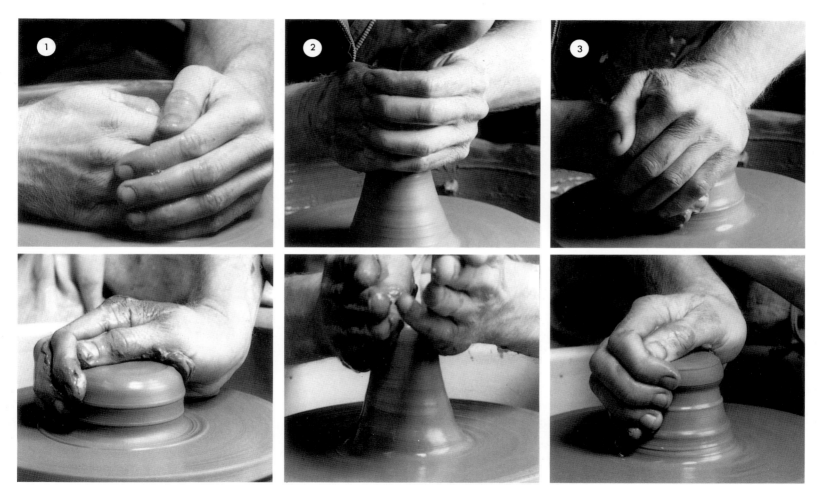

*Centring.*

lever, the clay can spring back out of centre. Instead, loosen your grip by gently relaxing your hand muscles.

● *The rim of the clay seems to be on centre but its stem is oscillating.* The 'mould' hand must be more rigid, like a claw, with the fingertips cutting in and down to the wheelhead. The fingers need stronger bracing from the gripping hand.

● *The clay stubbornly retains a persistent wobble.* Tuck your elbow into your hip or stomach and use your body weight to push your 'mould' hand against the clay. The clay may be too hard.

## CENTRED SHAPES FOR DIFFERENT FORMS

The width of the centred clay must vary to suit the shape it will develop into: a narrow dome for a tall pot and a flat disc for a wide, shallow dish. In general, the width needs to remain constant from the point of completing the centring to completing the pot.

# CENTRING A LARGER WEIGHT OF CLAY

Once you can no longer enclose the clay within your hands, your method needs to alter (see illustration opposite).

*1 Begin by placing the clay on the wheelhead and, turning the wheel slowly, pat it into a rough cone. Its own weight will help to stick it down.*

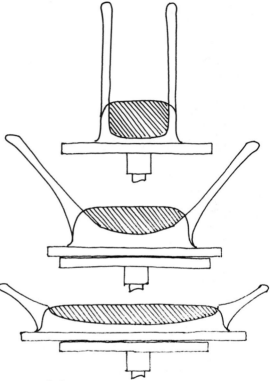

Centred shapes.

*2 Turn the wheel perhaps a little slower than your normal centring speed. Lubricate hands and clay. Leaning over the clay, point your elbows out and your forearms in, using your shoulder muscles to help your wrists and hands lift the clay into a tall cone. Grip with* your overlapping fingers as the cone narrows. Repeat as required.

*3 Standing over the clay, press from the top using your shoulder weight behind a vertical forearm, and control from the side. Again, grip with the overlapping hand. Concentrate on centring just the rim of the clay, as it compresses down.*

*4 Take care never to allow the clay to mushroom over at the edge, which traps air or slurry. This happens if the clay is not controlled from the side. The force applied from above should make the clay spread outwards from beneath your hands. Continue to flatten the clay to suit the form you are going to make.*

# THROWING A CYLINDRICAL FORM

In this most fundamental of exercises, the clay is centred, hollowed, opened out and pulled up into a vessel with a flat base and upright wall of even thickness. Any trimming or other finishing in the leather-hard state should be simply cosmetic rather than to carve away excess weight.

To achieve this becomes progressively more demanding and requires greater skills as you use more clay. It is sensible, therefore, for beginners to start with a manageable weight and build up the amount as your skill and confidence grow. Without weighing the pieces of clay you use, it is very difficult to gauge

Centring a larger weight of clay.

your progress, and easy to overestimate how much you need for a particular kind and size of vessel. Refer to the table on page 85 which lists items of functional ware and suggests weights to make them.

The sequence of photographs overleaf illustrates the growth of a simple cylinder. There are two pictures of each stage, one above the other. The lower one shows a cut-away view to allow close analysis of the action of the hands, and of the way the clay is distributed as the shape evolves.

## HOLLOWING OUT
### 1 Pushing down into the clay.
*This is done with fingers or thumb/s. You need to experiment to find an effective method for yourself which suits the role each hand wants to play. Remember that your hands are always aided by being linked in some way, here offering control and stability to the fingers making the hole, whilst braced against the outside of the clay.*

*Drop the speed a little, and take up a comfortable, steady position. Wet both hands and the clay, then form a slight dip in the centred dome to ensure that your hollow will be central, before pushing on down into the clay. Leave just enough thickness for the base: 3 – 5mm is ample for small vessels. Allow too much and your pots will gain weight and lose height.*

*Throwing a flat-based cylinder.*

### 2 Forming the flat base.

*As a continuation of the first move, the fingers or thumb/s now pull or stroke outwards to create an even, flat base undercutting the collar. Note how the fingers of the outside hand act as a buffer, giving control and counter-pressure, helping to restrict the width. Smoothing over and gently compressing the base once or twice helps to prevent cracking.*

## PULLING UP

### 3 The primary wall.

*Satisfy yourself that the base is smooth and flat before you proceed further. Once the wall is raised it is very awkward to reach. The cut-away picture shows that you have a broad tyre-shaped collar. This is now pinched and pulled upwards into a sturdy but even 'primary' wall.*

*If you pinch the clay as the wheel turns, you will create a groove. Now raise the pinch and the narrow aperture will draw and stretch the clay wall, making it thinner and taller. The wall's surface displays the characteristic spiral groove or 'throwing rings' – the hallmark of wheel-made pottery. The 'pinch' can be effected with numerous combinations of fingertips and knuckles, or with tools, but if the pressure is too slight, the wall will fail to rise. Again, experiment and practice are needed to evolve an effective method for yourself.*

*Here, the initial pull is carried out fingertip to fingertip. The thumb rests on the pads of the outside fingers as a steadying pivot. The upper body is leaning forward over the clay and the elbows are tucked in against it to stabilize the wrists and hands.*

### 4 Consolidating with a rib.

*With the primary wall raised, the throwing rib is an excellent aid in strengthening and straightening. Between pulling-up moves, it irons out deep throwing rings, shores up wobbles or weaknesses and cleans and dries the surface, allowing you to begin the next move with a 'clean slate'.*

## Lubrication

Lubricating the clay adequately is a key to smooth pulling up. Experienced potters use very little water, because the whole process is completed quickly and efficiently. However, more problems can arise from using too little water than too much. Dry patches will cause the fingers to drag or stick, breaking the all-important continuity of the action. Don't pour or splash water onto the pot; squeeze a wet sponge directly over the rim, coating the wall inside and out with a curtain of moisture, allowing the fingers to glide easily over the surface as your hands rise.

### 5 Pulling up to full height.

*Drop the wheel-speed a little more and lubricate the clay. Where the base of the wall meets the wheel, there is always a curving 'skirt' of clay. Cut this away with your fingertip to form a slight groove in which your knuckle can nestle. Inside the pot, your fingertips must be tucked right into the corner of the base. This position ensures that you will be utilizing all the clay to reach your target height.*

*To get an effective grip on the clay your fingers must face each other through the wall. Note how, here, it is the bony tip, not the fleshy pad of the inside fingers, which forms the 'pinch point' with the middle bone of the outside finger. This middle bone begins by sitting flat on the wheelhead, whilst the thumb rests on the back of the hand, forming the vital link which turns two hands into one stable tool.*

*Assume a comfortable and secure pose, leaning over the wheel, and raise your hands in smooth, unbroken moves from bottom to top. Experiment and lots of practice is required to find the body position, grip and speed that are right for you.*

### 6 Refining.

*Your aim should be to reach full height in as few moves as possible.*

*If you need to, consolidate with the rib and relubricate between pulls. Your pots can be thin-walled, but hold remarkable strength through being even in thickness and free from weak points. This is greatly enhanced by leaving a slight thickening on or just below the rim. It adds to the pot's wet strength, helping to prevent distortion when being handled, and in the kiln minimizes warping. To achieve this, the pressure in your pinch needs to be very gently relaxed as your hands rise past the halfway point or two-thirds of the wall's height.*

*Finally, the rib can be of practical help by cleaning and drying the surface, removing water and slurry, and by strengthening the wall. It may alter the character of the pot more than you wish, and is not essential, but may be used on selected areas to vary the quality of the surface in a decorative way.*

# FINISHING

Each pot you make can be tidied and refined significantly in the wet state, leaving minimal extra work when leather-hard or dry. These are three essentials which should become an automatic trio of refinements as you complete each pot.

## SPONGING OUT THE WATER

The puddle of water left inside the pot must be drained with a soft sponge (one tied to a stick is more practical and allows you to reach inside a deep, narrow pot). If this puddle is left it can cause the base to split during the subsequent uneven drying between wall and base.

## CHAMOISING THE RIM

Your completed pot will often have a squared, slurry-coated and untidy rim. The rim is the focal point of your pot and a crisp, clean, finished rim will improve the quality of that pot. It may seem natural and effective to do this with a sponge, but when examined

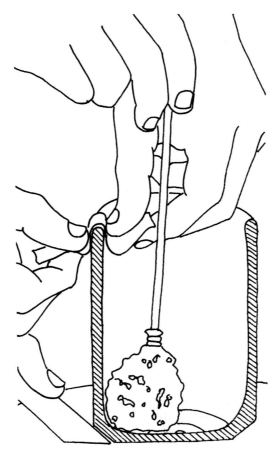

*Finishing refinements.*

closely, you will find that this causes the grog or sand in the body to be revealed and will leave it rough to the touch. A narrow strip of wet chamois leather (or even a strip of thin polythene) can be lightly pinched around the rim and this will push the grog into the surface and leave a polished film of slip.

## BEVELLING

At the base of your pot, where it joins the wheelhead, you will always get a curved, flaring skirt. If left in place and wired through, this creates an untidy, jagged edge encircling the base, and a 'suction pad' effect when you attempt to lift off your pot.

A neat undercut with a sharp, bevelled tool finishes your pot with simple efficiency. Done well, it requires a mere thumb around at the leather-hard stage to soften the base edge. Avoid using a metal tool against a metal wheelhead for this job – this blunts your tools and wears a depression in the wheelhead over time.

# CUTTING OFF

Unless you are using a bat, the pot must be wired through and either slid or lifted off. Learners often wire the pot through with water several times and slide it on an aquaplane to the edge of the wheelhead onto a hand or a waiting bat. For made-in-one flat-based forms, this makes a sticky mess of the bottom and can distort the form badly. Following a few simple steps, you can learn to lift the wet pot off the wheel and place it on a board, saving time and drying space.

*(See right, top row)*
*1 Towel dry your palms. Wire through with a fine twisted wire (keep the wire taut).*
*2 Without delay, gently cup your palms around the pot, low down on the wall (the tacky clay will adhere to your hands very lightly), lift away and place on a board.*

Avoid retouching the surface – the glaze will always cover the slight handprints. Correct any distortion at the leather-hard stage.

This procedure is easy with small cylindrical forms, but with practice can also be used for quite large pots with confidence.

As an aid, a sheet of newsprint can be used as a temporary airtight seal on the rim of your vessel, thus creating an effective resistance to the pressure of your hands as you hold and lift.

*(See right, bottom row)*
*1 Place a sheet of fresh, uncreased paper (a page from an old telephone directory is ideal) carefully on the rim of your pot.*
*2 Turn the wheel slowly and apply gentle finger pressure on the rim through the paper, creating a damp, unbroken ring.*

Now follow the cutting and lifting procedure and peel back the paper. The tacky disc of clay left on the wheelhead is an ideal glue on which to stick your next piece of clay.

Problems occur when your pots are *very* thin, particularly at the rim, or if your

*Cutting and lifting off.*

throwing is very uneven, or if the pot has taken a long time to throw and the clay has become soft and 'tired'. In these situations the pot may cave in. If the pot refuses to come unstuck, wire through again and lift immediately. Ribbing the surface free from water and slurry helps to stop it slipping out of your hands.

# REPAIRS

### COLLARING IN
Your throwing action may cause the form to flare more widely than you intend. It is good practice to keep the form narrower than you want until you complete the pot, as it is always easier to increase than decrease its diameter. Provided the pot is not already too thin-walled, it may be collared in.

*1 Put your thumbtips together and encircle the pot with your forefingers.*
*2 Close the aperture by progressively sliding one finger over the other as you simultaneously bring your hands up the wall. If the wall is already too thin, it will tend to buckle.*

### TRIMMING OFF A DAMAGED OR UNEVEN RIM
*1 Turn the wheel slowly and with a needle held in a steady hand, cut beneath the damaged section.*
*2 Hold a finger lightly against the inside and as the needle meets it, lift away the unwanted collar.*

*Collaring and trimming. (Left) collaring in (Right) trimming the rim.*

## AIR BUBBLES

Poor preparation may leave air pockets in your clay, which, during throwing, can appear as bumps or blisters in the clay wall. Too many of these will mean having to re-wedge your clay, but the odd blister can simply be punctured with a needle before being smoothed over.

# COMMON FAULTS

The simplest and most graphic way to analyse your results on the wheel is to examine them in cross-section. With your wire, cut halfway through the base and bring it up vertically through the wall. The remaining half reveals just how well the clay has been distributed, shows where faults have occurred, and indicates how to correct them. The diagrams on the right are of some of the most typical cross-sections you may find.

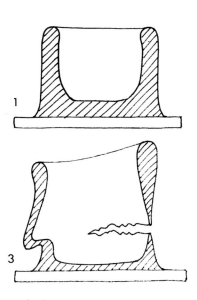

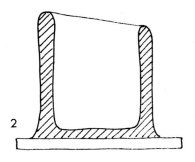

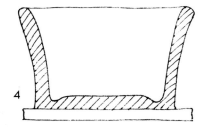

*Common faults.*

**1 Stunted height.**
*Effect* – pot is short, thick and heavy.
*Cause* – base has not been thinned or flattened enough and the wall has only been partially thrown.
*Remedy* – ensure the base is thin, flat and wide enough prior to pulling up. Adjust your pinching and pulling when making the wall.

**2 Off centre.**
*Effect* – rim uneven in height and walls uneven in thickness.
*Cause* – hollowing out was begun before clay was sufficiently centred.

*Remedy* – improve your centring technique. A mild unevenness may be trimmed up with a needle.

**3 Sheared or collapsing wall.**
*Effect* – clay literally tears, buckles or collapses in your hands.
*Causes* – over-effective grip when pulling up, creating overthinned or overworked wall and/or lack of lubrication, causing clay to stick to hands and tear.

*Remedy* – relax pulling grip slightly, use a rib to strengthen and consolidate the wall between pulls, lubricate before each pull.

**4 Flaring.**
*Effect* – pot flares and widens instead of standing tall and straight.
*Causes* – failure to keep centred clay narrow at outset. Throwing action and speed of wheel pulls wall out instead of up, or wall is allowed to collapse outwards at its base.

*Remedy* – keep form tapered in initial stage by collaring in when necessary. Remember the rule: keep the form narrower than you intend to finish with. Alter your throwing position by leaning over the clay and pulling up more vertically.

## TO MEASURE THE BASE THICKNESS

Stop the wheel. Push a needle through the base to the wheelhead. Run a fingertip down the needle to the clay. Holding the fingertip in place, pull out and measure the tip of the needle exposed. Smooth over the prick mark.

*Measuring the base thickness.*

*The author at work in his studio, decorating leather-hard pots.*

# CHAPTER THREE

# DEVELOPMENT OF FORMS

There are many forms that potters make that would simply spoil, distort or collapse if you attempted to cut and remove them by hand. Wide, flat forms such as dishes and plates, awkward forms like bowls, and very large or delicate fine wares all benefit from having their own rigid base upon which they can be thrown and lifted from the wheel to dry untouched. To do this a removable base or bat must be secured firmly to the wheelhead. There are numerous devices on which to slot a compatible bat, but it is useful to learn how to fix any bat to any wheelhead using a clay pad.

## BATS

Bats can be made from several kinds of material, their most important property being the ability to remain flat through constant wetting and drying.

Plywood and chipboard are commonly used. Chipboard will swell and break down if it is left immersed in water, but it is cheap, does not warp and will last well if looked after.

A thicker material will remain rigid and warp less easily than a thin one. A minimum for chip or ply is 12 mm.

## Problems

The bat will come unstuck, or slide during throwing if:
(a) the pad is too wet, too dry, humped or uneven, too narrow for the bat or too thick;
(b) the bat is too wet, warped, coated in dust or dry clay, or if the surface is pitted or cracked;
(c) the throwing clay is stiff and put under excessive horizontal pressure during centring, or thrown using too little lubrication.

## BAT CARE

Wire through beneath your pots well before they are too stiff, and remove them when appropriate to do so. Immediately scrape your bats clean, as doing so when the clay 'skin' is dry can damage the surface. Be sure to discard these scrapings. They may be contaminated with wood chips, so should not be added to recycled clay.

## Fixing a bat

*1 Use well-prepared clay, slightly on the stiff side (300–500 g for a bat 20–30 cm [8–12 in]). Centre a shallow disc at normal speed.*
*2 Thin and flatten further, controlling the edge as it widens, taking care not to allow air or slurry to be folded underneath. Pad width should be 20–30 mm narrower than your bat, thickness 5–10 mm.*
*3 Use a rib to smooth and dry the surface. Ensure that the pad is quite flat and without the slightest hump in the centre.*
*4 Using a right-angled edge, score spiral or concentric grooves, and a cross across the width. Be sure to leave a level ridge between the grooves (the cross allows an escape for air to prevent the bat becoming bonded by vacuum suction).*
*5 The pad should be free from surface water. Sponge off if necessary. Take a clean, dry bat which overlaps the pad by at least 10–20 mm and moisten with a damp sponge on the underside. Do not wet.*
*6 Place the bat on the pad and centre up. Turn the wheel slowly and thump the bat*

*Fixing a bat.*

*centrally with a fist or rolling-pin end (not on one side or the pad will distort). After the pot is made, sponge around the bat and lever off (do not wire off). Provided the pad is kept moist, it will remain usable. Cover with a sheet of polythene to preserve for any length of time.*

## TALL FORMS

For plastic clay to stand up tall and thin, it needs to be firm enough to support its own weight. This means striking a balance between this need and your ability to centre and hollow out, which is easier if the clay is softer. This also means using less water on the clay, which implies reaching your goal height in as few pulls as you can. Constant wetting and lifting makes the clay soggy and tired until it refuses to rise any more. Smooth clays may become weak and flabby, so using a clay body with a suitable filler, such as fine sand or grog, gives increased wet strength without the disadvantage of making the clay too coarse.

It is sensible to build up your weight of clay gradually. Using every gram of even 0·5–1 kg will take considerable skill and practice. Using more than you can cope with will result in disheartening dumpy, heavy pots, sapping your confidence and quickly using up your carefully prepared clay. The method used is shown in the sequence of photographs opposite.

*1 Centre, hollow out and form a good flat base in the usual way. Make sure the diameter is as narrow as your intended pot. Allowing the base to widen too much at this stage will sacrifice height. Raise the primary wall as high and as evenly as possible (perhaps one-half to two-thirds of the target height).*
*2 To help keep the form as narrow as you can, it is a useful move to collar in the primary wall to a more tapered shape. Having done so, rib the surface to consolidate and strengthen in preparation for your next long pull up.*
*3 To continue pulling up the clay, a higher position over the wheel is needed. Reduce the speed of the wheel and make sure that the walls are evenly lubricated. Lean over the wheel with straightened arms in a secure standing position. Cut a groove at the base of the outside wall with a finger for your knuckle to settle into, form an effective pinch and pull up. Raise your hands initially by straightening your back.*
*4 Should your fingers slip out of alignment, steady and straighten the wall with a rib. Rib the full height before and after each pull. As the wall thins it may want to ripple or twist, so take care not to let your fingers dry and drag. Again, careful use of the rib will iron out most of the wobbles you encounter.*
*5 Constant wetting and pulling will eventually saturate and weaken the wall. A key to success is economy and efficiency. Allow yourself less time to complete each pull*

*and then measure the height to check your progress.*
*6 Rib dry and complete refinement (sponge, chamois, bevel – see page 23).*

## BOTTLE FORMS

Achieve maximum height first, with the top section sloping in from the point where the shoulder will be. Use the collaring technique to close in the form slowly, leaving sufficient weight at the rim to create a decent neck on the pot.

## BELLIED FORMS

It is a classically natural thing for a thrown pot to have a curvaceous, distended form. Gentle pressure from inside, and the wheel's centrifugal force, are all that are required to increase a vessel's volume greatly for its weight. Potters down the centuries have made functional everyday vessels with simple, graceful curves and little or no surface decoration, illustrating how a strong form can hold enough presence as an object without further embellishment.

Each pot you make must have a basic form which holds the important elements of height and width (at both base and rim) from which it can be converted. You could regard them as the primary and secondary forms. See overleaf for an explanation of the method used.

*Throwing a taller form.*

*1 Lightly lubricate the interior and exterior of the wall, turn the wheel slowly and begin to stroke out the shape from the base of the wall.*
*2 As the hand moves up inside, the fingers or rib follow on the outside offering gentle counter-pressure.*
*3 The eye should be concentrating on the quality of the curve. Don't try to extend the belly to its full girth in one movement. Repeat steps (1), (2) and (3) in several upward sweeps.*
*4 A metal kidney flexed into a curve can act as a profile to smooth the surface and line of the belly.*

## Tips
● Visually the form will look lighter and less dumpy if the widest point of the girth comes slightly above halfway up the height of the belly.
● Forms with a narrow neck may require a bellying rib to reach down inside and push out the shape.
● If the primary form is uneven or off-centre, such a weakness will be further stressed and exaggerated and is likely to cause the form to collapse.

*Bellying out the form.*

*Burnished-earthenware jar form by Duncan Ross. On a narrow, turned base, 23 cm high. Photo Duncan Ross.*

*Throwing a flat plate.*

# WIDE, FLAT FORMS

The great advantage in making anything wide and flat is being able to use much softer clay, so the centring becomes less of a chore. There is a very little or no pulling up involved and therefore no problems with wobbling or collapsing walls.

However, the different process introduces new problems. A bat will have to be used for each pot or plate and unless securely fixed will create a new source of frustration. Flat wares use a lot of clay in the making and are more vulnerable to drying cracks, so good clay preparation is particularly important in this case.

The example illustrated opposite is of a simple flat plate. Note how the centred clay is no longer a dome or even a shallow hump, but a wide, flat disc.

*1 As the edge of the hand pressures out the clay, the key action of the hidden hand is to control the edge as it expands, with fingertips pressed together and against the disc rim (note the thumb braced on top of the wrist).*
*2 A shallow well is sunk into the centre of the disc and the width is further increased, whilst the thumb hooked onto the outer edge again prevents the clay folding over like a mushroom to envelop air and slurry.*
*3 A similar action again as the correct thickness of base is reached (check with a pin: 5–7 mm for a dinner plate).*

*4 The weight of both hands smooths and compresses the base making it even and increasing crack resistance.*
*5 The sponge-dried plate is smoothed with a rib.*
*6 Finally, the rim is given character and refinements prior to chamois and bevel.*

## CUTTING OFF THE BAT
Ideally, leave wet plates to 'go off' slightly (*never* leather-hard) before cutting through. This will help prevent them re-adhering. Take great care to keep the wire taut and flat on the bat as you pull the wire through.

*Vases by the author (larger vases thrown in two sections). Slip-decorated earthenware, 33, 15 and 22 cm high.*

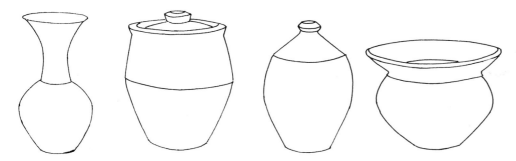

*Sectional forms.*

# SECTIONAL FORMS

As your skills improve, so does your ambition. It takes a long time to develop the technique of raising the clay taller and thinner, and aspiring throwers may for long periods feel trapped on a skills plateau, where the addition of extra weights of clay refuses to be converted into extra height. By throwing with smaller weights of clay, which gives greater control, and with accurate measuring, you can make a piece in sections and join them together. Certain forms lend themselves particularly well to this technique, for example where a form has a crisp change of angle, enclosed bottle shapes, or narrow-necked vases and jugs rising from a wide, rounded belly.

*Tall-necked jug by the author. Two thrown sections joined together, with pulled handle applied leather-hard. Slip-decorated earthenware, 35 cm high.*

## METHOD

Throw the bottom section, taking care to keep it as well centred as you can. An uneven or undulating rim causes problems during the joining. Give the rim a square profile and, as usual, a little extra weight. With callipers, measure across the *inside* edge so that they just touch at either side. (Do this at several points around the circumference in case the rim is distorted into an oval, and compensate accordingly.) Do *not* wire through!

The top section is a cylinder without a base, and in effect is thrown upside-down. It is usually the smaller of the two sections so will need rather less clay in the making. Centre the clay to a shape that can develop into the correct form, then hollow right down to the bat's surface. Draw out the collar as if you were making a wide, shallow dish. Now pull up the wall, creating a rim of the same width and weight as the bottom section, measuring as carefully as you can. Bevel the bottom of the wall both inside and outside.

## JOINING TWO SECTIONS

*1 Obviously the bottom half, which is taking the weight, will need to stiffen up somewhat before the two sections are joined, but how much depends on how much more shaping needs to be carried out. The top section, once joined, can continue to be thrown and refined, so will most often need to remain soft enough to do so. The two sections are thrown and measured.*

*Joining two sections.*

2 Sponge and thoroughly score the rim of the top section. Re-centre the bottom section (on its bat) and fix firmly. A clay pad is usually quite adequate for this, provided it is not too dry. Now score and slurry its rim.

3 Invert the top section and lower carefully into place, aligning the edges as best you can. Turn the wheel slowly, and examine how central it is. Carefully lift off and re-centre if necessary. Tap the bat lightly in the centre to seat in the join.

4 Using a metal kidney or table knife, turn the wheel and lightly seal the outside join.

5 To cut off the bat, take a taut wire through, pressing it up against the underside of the bat at each side with a fingertip. It helps to lean in with your chest against the bat for counter-pressure.

6 Lift off the bat.

7 Now gently turning the wheel, align the join inside and out with the fingers, then trim and refine with a metal kidney.

8 Once securely joined, you may now further trim, refine and shape the top section. If you find you have too much weight of clay to complete your form, trim the rim with a needle. If you wish to add further sections, shape the rim and measure accordingly.

# CHAPTER FOUR

# CURVED-BASE FORMS

## THROWING CURVED-BASE FORMS

Archaeological collections in museums are filled with beautiful and simple pottery vessels made for very practical uses such as fetching and carrying, cooking and storage. Rows of tall, enclosed bottles and wide, open bowls all sit on discreet devices allowing the onlooker to admire their completely rounded forms. These objects were made for an environment without our smooth, flat, horizontal surfaces, and will sit happily upright on earth or sand or straddling a tripod of stones. Spherical or hemi-spherical forms are both structurally and aesthetically strong, and the potter's desire to re-create such shapes is as potent as ever.

For throwers, this involves a second distinct process, that of paring away the excess clay at the base in the semi-dry or 'leather-hard' state. This process is known as *trimming* or *turning*, and this chapter deals with forms that need to be treated in this way in order to complete the object.

## BOWLS AND DISHES

Perhaps the most significant difference in the approach to throwing open-formed bowls and dishes, as compared with enclosed upright wares, is in the focus on the interior surface and profile rather than on the exterior surface and silhouette. The shallower the form becomes, the more this is the case, and proportionately the more clay you will need to support the overhanging wall.

The drawings below show a variety of bowl shapes. The left-hand side of each depicts a shaded cross-section of the trimmed form with a line enclosing a stippled area to indicate the original outline and thickness of the pot when thrown. The right-hand side depicts the exterior of the completed form.

The curved interiors are faithfully followed on the exterior, leaving only a shallow collar or 'footring' on which the form stands. The width, weight and quality of the footring has

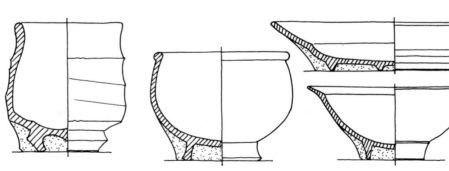

*Curved-base forms.*

*Porcelain bowl by Lucie Rie. Photo courtesy of* Ceramic Review.

to relate sympathetically with the bowl. Too narrow, and the shape can overbalance, or slump, in the kiln. Too broad, and the bowl will look and feel heavy.

## BASIC BOWL

This form is neither shallow nor deep. The clay needs to be of medium consistency.

*1 The centred clay is a shallow hump. Note that at the base the clay remains a similar width throughout. Hollow down to footring depth – here approx 10mm – and draw your flat fingertips across to create a curved base and undercut beneath the collar. The thumb rests on the pads of the fingers, which are keeping a gentle counter-pressure on the outside, preventing the width from increasing.*
*2 Slow the wheel, lubricate the wall inside and out, tuck your fingers well into the base of the outer wall and pull the primary wall upwards and outwards. Concentrate on keeping a good flowing curve from the base into the wall. Wrap the fingertips around the rim as you complete each pull to steady and consolidate.*
*3 Slow the wheel further still to pull up the secondary, finished height. Note how on this form about half the height of the wall is fully thinned, requiring trimming only from halfway down. To widen the form, gently fold out the rim to the width you want.*

*Throwing a basic bowl.*

**4** *The rib is then used to smooth and refine the curve from the centre up into the wall. Support the wall outside with following fingers.*

### Bowl making – common faults

Beginning with the base too narrow (A) is the most common cause of problems when making bowls. Without a wide foundation the walls will very often droop outwards causing a 'ski jump' (B) on the slope of the interior, or collapse. A thin or weak point (C) may also cause a collapse, often caused by the clay being off-centre. Failure to create a nicely curving base breaks up the line of the bowl's interior and may leave a thin point (D). As the bowl's diameter is widened, its rim thins considerably, so unless the primary wall's rim is thick enough, the finished rim will be weak and thin (E) and prone to damage or warping.

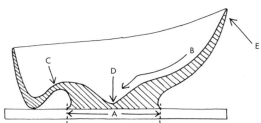

*Common faults when throwing bowls.*

# THROWING A WIDER AND SHALLOWER BOWL

To support a wide, overhanging wall, the centred clay must be flatter and wider still. Form a subtle, curving base as before, using the full width of the centred clay.

*1 On this wide foundation, the primary and secondary walls are raised, using a progressively gentler speed, at a shallower sloping angle. Do not overthin the wall or rim at this stage.*
*2 At a very gentle pace the rim is eased outwards like a slight trumpet mouth. Here the straight edge of the rib reinforces and steadies the outer wall.*
*3 Now working from the centre of the bowl, the rib's curved profile regains the sweeping concave curve of the interior whilst the other hand prevents the rim from falling further outwards.*
*4 Steps (2) and (3) may be repeated several times before your width and shape are achieved. Refine in the usual way.*

*Throwing a wider, shallower bowl.*

# SHALLOW DISH WITH A WIDE RIM

*(See overleaf for sequence photographs)*

Although the dish illustrated appears flat, it actually has a gentle and very shallow curve. The preparation needed and beginnings of the making process are very similar to those for the flat form illustrated on page 34. Although this is a shallow, curving shape supported by an almost solid base, it requires a lot of clay, with plenty of trimming at a later stage.

*1 A wide and shallow disc is centred out, using the width of the bat. Remember to keep control of the edge as the disc widens.*
*2 A shallow well is pressed into the disc centre. This is the thinnest point of the base and does not need a significant allowance for trimming (8–12 mm depending on the dish width). The fingers draw out the gentle curve whilst the thumb hooks over the rim to prevent mushrooming.*
*3 Take the base thickness down a little more and create a thick collar on the outer edge. Use the weight of both hands to smooth and compress the base.*
*4 Rib off the centre.*
*5 The rim travels considerably faster on a wide form, so it is essential to slow the wheel right down to pull the rim up and out. Take care not to over-thin as this will weaken it badly during the next step. Allow plenty of*

The author at the wheel, ribbing out the final form of a large, wide bowl.

*Throwing a dish with a wide rim.*

*weight beneath the rim for support when it is flattened out.*

**6** *Drop the speed to a virtual crawl (10–15 r p m) and very, very gently fold down the rim, keeping a finger beneath the very edge to prevent it going down too far. Some potters like to allow this rim to dry a little before it is taken down to its shallowest angle.*

The keys to preventing a terminal collapse are good support, good centring, even throwing and slow execution. When removing a wide-rimmed form from the wheel, never set down with a jolt, as this may cause the rim to flop. Wire through well before the clay stiffens.

*Note* A rim with a slight upward tilt is much less likely to droop in the kiln than a horizontal one.

*Dish with wide rim by the author. Slip-decorated earthenware, 45 cm wide.*

# CHAPTER FIVE

# TRIMMING AND TURNING

## DRYING YOUR POTS

Confusion can arise over the vague terminology that potters use to describe the condition of the clay. A clear understanding of this language is important because different stages of the making process come at crucial stages in the drying cycle.

The knack lies in getting the clay to the state you need at a convenient time. The pot is drying from the moment you finish it. In a warm, dry, well-ventilated atmosphere, the water evaporates out of the clay much more quickly than in cool, humid, airless conditions. The thin extremities, such as the rim, will dry first. This is indicated by a change in the clay's colour – it begins to lighten. But this is undesirable when there is further work to do on the pot, so ways to even-up or equalize the drying must be employed.

As soon as a rim is stiff enough, turn the pot over and allow the base to get an airing. With wide shapes thrown on a bat, another clean bat should be placed on the rim and the pot inverted, sandwiched in between the two bats. Now you may remove the bat from the base. Alternatively, the rim may be sealed in plastic to retard the drying process. There are fireproofing sheet materials with super-absorbency. These can be cut into planks and used as pot-drying boards, which equalize the drying top and bottom. An airtight, damp cupboard or humidified room where pots can be stored, untouched, to dry evenly, will preserve more delicate items.

Problems can arise when you are unable to check the pots every day, as with weekly classes. Wrap up a wet pot and it remains too wet; leave it uncovered and it is often much too dry. Cut circles of thin plastic that will just cover the rim. As the outside dries, it slowly draws the moisture from the sealed interior.

To accelerate the process, a pot may be force-dried using an electric fan heater; faster still, using a gas blowlamp or paint-stripping gun. Slowly revolve the pot on a turntable or on the wheel and wave the hot air or flame over the surface. Keep fingering the pot to check its condition. Once a pot is in an ideal state, seal it completely in its own plastic bag. Kitchen binliners or bags are ideal.

## LEATHER-HARD CLAY

What does the term 'leather-hard' mean? When is a pot in this state?

As the term 'plastic' is used to describe the clay's condition for throwing, 'leather-hard' is the term most often used to describe its condition for all the remaining finishing processes – applying handles, lugs, knobs and spouts, trimming and turning.

Clay in the semi-dry state becomes more rigid but still slightly pliable – similar to thick leather or hide. It allows you to handle the pot safely without distortion, whilst remaining moist enough to graft on appendages and soft enough to carve into. Within the term, though, the clay will vary from being soft like Cheddar cheese to hard like chocolate. To look at, the clay should still appear a uniform colour.

### DRYING FOR FIRING

Once a piece is complete, it may be left uncovered to air-dry completely. However, drying cracks can occur in certain circumstances.

*Reduced stoneware bowl by Janice Tchalenko. Sponged glaze decoration, 25 cm wide. Photo Tim Hill.*

**Typical causes**
- Poor joins of any kind, but especially handles, lugs or knobs (usually where the pot was already too dry for effective joining).
- Weak, thin or delicate points in a wall, base or appendage.
- Puddles of water left inside.

## RECLAIMING THE CLAY

Clay that has passed the plastic state should be allowed to dry completely before soaking in water. Break or cut thick lumps into small or thin pieces for quicker drying. (Lumps of plastic or leather-hard clay only break down very slowly. Small pieces of dry clay disintegrate like an aspirin tablet.)

Once soaked, drain off the surface water and lay out the slurry on an absorbent slab to become dry enough to re-wedge. Take care not to contaminate your reclaim with foreign bodies. Discard floor sweepings.

As you work, pots which collapse or which you don't wish to keep can be allowed to stiffen a little and re-wedged or used wet to soften another batch of clay.

# TRIMMING AND TURNING

When is a pot ready to turn? It is not easy to give a definitive answer to this question because the needs of different shapes and sizes of forms, types of clay and wares and personal preferences of potters are all too variable to sum up in a universal rule.

The answer 'when it is leather-hard' is too general. A better rule to apply would be 'as soon as the pot is stiff enough to work on, providing the desired quality of finish, without becoming distorted or damaged'. As a general guide, the base area to be turned should be soft enough to mark with a thumbnail but not so soft as to make an impression with a fingertip. The trimmings should have the consistency of grated cheese which when squeezed in the hand will just stick together. If the trimmings are crumbly like grated chocolate, the clay is already on the borderline, and if they are like iron filings, it is too dry.

## TURNING A FOOTRING

To assess how much clay must be pared away before turning a bowl it is helpful to make a couple of markers and measurements to guide you (see opposite).

*1 Sit the bowl upright on a flat surface and stand a measuring stick vertically against the rim. Mark the rim height (A). Now stand the stick in the bottom of the bowl, look across the bowl, lining up the near and far rims at eye level, and mark that point too (B). The difference between the marks gives the base thickness at its thinnest point.*
*2 Look down the line of the wall (C), run a finger and thumb down and mark with a thumbnail where they begin to diverge, i.e. where the wall begins to thicken (D).*

*3 On the underside of the bowl, mark where the outside edge of the footring will come with another thumbnail mark (E). (The diameter of the footring will vary according to the shape, width and style of each bowl, but a practical average might be one-third to one-half of the rim's diameter.)*
*4 Lastly, and most importantly, study the curve and line of the interior. It is this that you are aiming to reproduce and should be kept in your mind's eye once the bowl is turned over.*

# FIXING THE BOWL TO THE WHEEL

*(See illustration, far right)*

## Method 1

*Centre the bowl upside-down on the wheelhead or on a wider bat and hold firmly in place with three short coils of plastic clay, taking care not to distort the rim. For checking progress, pin prick on one coil and just above on the bowl, remove one coil and slide the pot out. Slide back and align pin pricks, and stick back third coil. This method is suitable for one-off sizes of bowl, taller, deeper forms and those with sturdy rims.*

## Method 2

*Stick a coil of plastic clay on the wheel, approximately the same diameter as the pot, and with a turning tool trim into a shallow*

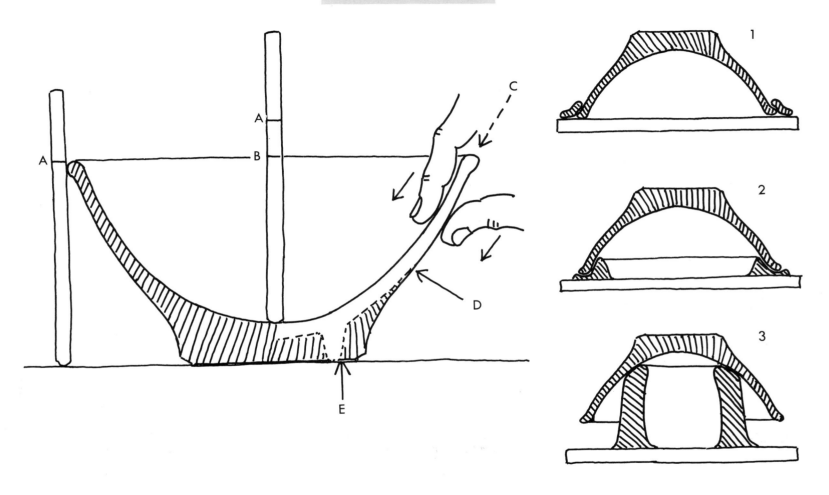

*Measuring for turning a footring.*

*Methods of fixing the bowl to the wheel.*

collar on which the rim can be stuck. This method is ideal for easy centring, repeats of the same size and small- to medium-sized pots.

## Method 3

*Throw a thick clay collar or 'chuck' and allow this to dry to stiff leather-hard, or stick a solid block of stiff clay to the wheel and trim to size with a turning tool. Angle the edge of the chuck to match the curve of the bowl. Centre the bowl upside-down on the chuck (level up the base with a small spirit-level if necessary) and tap or press to stick. If it fails to stick, re-moisten chuck. This method is suitable for uneven, carved or delicate rims, to trim a number of bowls of one size, or shallow, wide or large forms.*

## TURNING

### Tapping into centre

*1 Place your pot as close to centre as you can. Revolve the wheel holding a steady fingertip level with the base and close enough so that the pot brushes the finger on the widest point of its trajectory.*

  *Count '1-2-1-2-1' each time it touches to pick up the rhythm, then tap the pot towards the axis of the wheel on the beat '1-2'. Tap slightly in the direction of spin. If the pot is small and light, with the other hand use a light finger pressure on top of the pot to act as a brake. Practise with a plastic bowl for a couple of minutes every session. Focus the eye*

Turning a footring.

on the edge of the base (where the turning is to be done), not on the rim of the pot (where it is not).

2 Hold the pot firmly whilst you press the clay coils into place.

3 Find your marker on the base and cut a groove to establish the width of the footring. Note how the fingers of the left hand bridge the pot and tool throughout, acting as a stabilizer.

4 Mark the second starting point on the wall. Your turning will take place between these boundaries. The speed of the wheel should be brisk, not slow. Concentrate on keeping the tool hand firm and still.

5 Bearing in mind your measurement of the base thickness and memory of the interior curve, proceed to carve the depth and angle of the footring and –

6 – the slope of the wall. Note how the angle of the turning tool's blade is constantly adjusted.

7 Now trim out the hollow inside the footring, taking care to continue the curve of the form and giving the footring a similar weight, thickness and quality to the form's rim. To prevent too much downward pressure against the base, use the tool at a very shallow angle. A shallow bevel to the inside and outside edges of the footring and a smooth with a firm fingertip gives a functional and neat refinement.

8 To assess your work, pick up the bowl and rock it from side to side in your cradled hands. It should feel balanced, its weight

*being evenly distributed, not bottom-heavy. Run a thumb and forefinger down either side of the wall to feel for thicknesses and compare the interior and exterior curves.*

## TRIMMING A TALL, CYLINDRICAL POT

*(See illustration, right)*
*1 To secure a tall pot, the fixing coils must be broader, like buttresses. Unless the trimming needed is only minor, you may need to take some measurements such as the interior base width and wall thickness before you begin.*
*2 The full width of the turning tool's blade is used to create a smooth, clean surface. The stabilizing fingers straddling pot and tool are particularly important in preventing the pot from suddenly breaking loose and being damaged.*

## TURNING A WIDE, SHALLOW FORM

To handle a wide form safely during the trimming stage, it is necessary to allow the clay to dry a little harder than for a small object. This enables the finished form to hold its shape after trimming.

Measure starting points for turning the rim and footring in the same way as for bowls,

and if your form has a ledge between rim and dish, it is useful to make a third mark above this. See opposite for sequence illustrations.

*1 A wide chuck will have to be used. The chuck should have a similar width to the footring. Centre up.*
*2 Mark off your starting points on the rim and footring, then, if relevant, your third marker to establish the rim's width and thickness. You can stop and check this with thumb and forefinger.*
*3 Finish and refine the form outside the footring. Depending on the thickness and width of the dish, at least one more inner support will be required. This may be merely a narrow pad, or a second, narrower ring. Whichever you choose, it is important not to leave the base too thin or too thick.*
*4 Mark off the diameter of the inner footring and use the point or corner of the tool to turn the bulk of the base thickness. This creates less downward pressure.*
*5 Use the broad blade to smooth off, taking care to follow the gentle curve of the base.*
*6 Finally, trim inside the inner footring.*

Generally speaking, thrown dishes tend to be heavy for their surface area, and vulnerable to warping and cracking, particularly in stoneware firings, if they are uneven in throwing or trimming.

Care must be taken in lifting off wide forms. They can be easily distorted. Lift one edge enough to slide an outstretched hand underneath the centre of the form. Turn it

*Trimming a tall pot.*

*Turning a wide dish.*

*Bowl by Takeshi Yasuda. The flat 'sprung' base has been pressed out into a bowl shape. Sansai glaze, oxidized stoneware. Photo Takeshi Yasuda.*

over and place on a flat surface to dry – a bat is ideal. Very large and wide forms may need to be removed with the chuck. Place a bat on the trimmed base and invert chuck and dish together, then lift off the chuck.

# TURNING – COMMON FAULTS

*A classic example* (*see right*): the curve of the outside wall does not follow the line of the interior. This creates an uneven thickness (A) and (B), and a weak point (C), where the pot may split or slump in the kiln. The thickness and weight of the footring is too square (D) and bulky (E) for the bowl's size, and its width (F) is perhaps too narrow. Inside the footring the base has been trimmed flat, again failing to follow the interior line and causing a bump (G) with a weakened or cracked rim.

## CHATTERING
When the pot is getting dry, the turning tool 'chatters' or vibrates on the surface, causing ridges. Dampen the surface with a sponge and continue.

## CUTTING THROUGH
This is usually caused by creating a weak point through inaccurate or careless measuring. But a student who is 'scared to go too far in case they cut through' inevitably ends up making unsatisfactory heavy pots by playing safe.

# TURNING TALL, NARROW-NECKED OR AWKWARD FORMS

If it is not possible to stand a pot on its rim, you will have to create a special chuck or collar (see below). These can be kept in a leather-hard state or biscuit-fired, and edged with soft clay when in use.

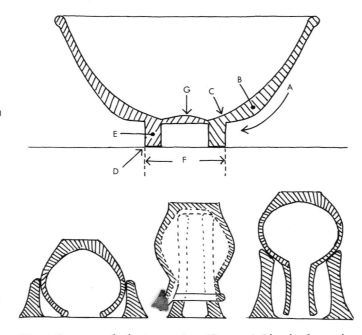

*(Top) Common faults in turning. (Bottom) Chucks for awkward forms.*

# CHAPTER SIX

# LIPS AND HANDLES

## JUGS: FORMING A POURING LIP

We have already looked at the need for extra weight at the rims of your pots to prevent them warping. This is of greater significance when you are creating lips and applying handles. The rim, collar or shoulder of your form needs to be subtly stronger still. The way you form a pouring lip depends on the shape and character of the jug.

### On a rolled or collared rim (see opposite, top row)

*1 Here the rim will first have to be refined on the section where the lip is to be pulled. Wet a thumb and crooked forefinger and gently thin and stretch the rim using a light grip and upward strokes.*
*2 The grip moves from side to side creating an upstanding curve (the edge of the curve may need to be refined with a light stroke of the chamois leather or between forked fingers).*
*3 Now the lip and throat can be formed using the usual method.*

### On a ready-refined rim (see opposite, bottom row)

*1 The thumb and forefinger of one hand form the aperture (width to match pot). These need to be towel-dried to make them adhere slightly to the rim. The forefinger of the other hand is kept wet and, pointing down into the pot, begins to stroke or waggle from side to side, gently stretching the clay into a U shape.*
*2 The finger can incorporate a movement up and down into the neck of the pot to create a 'throat'.*
*3 The lip can be given further emphasis by gently folding either side back against the thumb and forefinger to turn the U into a C.*

### Tips

Form the lip as you complete each pot, even whilst it is still on the wheel. If the pot has begun to dry, the action may cause the rim to split. Correct any distortions by gently pushing either side of the lip – if it appears off-centred, for instance.
*Note* If the rim is already thin and weak, the action of lip-forming may distort the pot irrevocably during making or kiln-firing.

The nature of clay is to want to unfold itself and return to its former shape, so it is useful to exaggerate the lip a little in the making.

## MAKING PULLED HANDLES

Of the various ways to form a handle, the pulled handle is arguably the most natural to use on a thrown pot. It is drawn from a stem of plastic clay with hand and water, acquiring the trademarks akin to wheel-made pottery. It can most readily be made to appear to grow organically from the pot, twisting and bending elastically to complement the curve and vitality of a strong thrown form. It may be applied wet, or pre-formed and applied in the leather-hard state.
*Note* It is essential that the clay you use to pull your handles is as well prepared as throwing clay and of a similar consistency. See overleaf for sequence illustrations and instructions.

*Pulling lips (Top row) on a rolled rim (Bottom row) on a refined rim.*

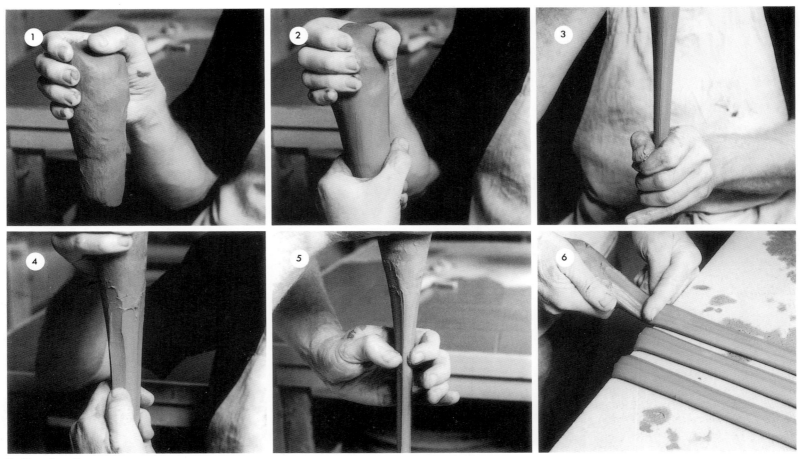

*Pulling handles.*

*1 Form a tapered stem of clay – enough to grasp comfortably in the palm of one hand – and hold over a bucket or bowl of water. Have ready a clean bench or board.*
*2 Wet both the pulling hand and the clay.*
*3 Begin to stroke and draw the clay, in darting, downward movements. The grip of your pulling hand will resemble that of milking a cow, but without the squeeze! The clay is gradually extended through the slight friction created, but keep re-wetting the hand to prevent the strip tearing off.*
*From here there are two options:*
*A A tapered stub is cut off to be later welded, end on, to the pot, being further pulled and refined from the pot itself.*
*B A parallel strap is fully shaped and refined, cut off and applied either wet or leather-hard as a pre-formed loop shape.*
*4 As the strap of clay extends, keep turning the stem between pulls to refine the back, front and edges of the handle.*
*5 Use the thumb and forefinger to flatten the shape and pinch the edges. If a weak point or kink is created on the length of the strap, pinch it off and draw more clay from the stem to lengthen the handle.*
*6 Lay the pieces down flat and cut them off cleanly with your finger. If the handles are to be joined wet, keep them covered in plastic until you are ready to use them. To pre-form the loop of a handle, use a cardboard tube or rolling pin to drape the straps over.*

# APPLYING A PARALLEL HANDLE

Assess the length of handle that you will need and trim the ends cleanly with a cutting wire. With a wet toothbrush, score both joining points on the pot, creating a rough, slurry-coated area.
*Note* The top join should be low enough not to allow the loop to rise higher than the pot rim. Stand the pot on the edge of the bench. (See illustrations, right.)

*1 Pick up the handle at one end with the good side facing into the pot. Hold vertically against the wall with the last 12 mm level with the scored area and pinch gently into place with the thumb and forefinger. Keep the handle held up straight whilst you use the thumb to weld the top join neatly.*
*2 Now place a finger slightly above the join and behind the handle, and lower the handle into a loop over the finger, lightly adhering the end to the scored area below. Check its position before the welding and cosmetic work.*

# PULLING A HANDLE FROM THE POT

*(See overleaf for sequence illustrations.)*
*1 Decide where the handle is to be fixed and score the area with a wet toothbrush. Take the handle stub and slightly flare the butt end*

*Applying a parallel handle.*

*Pulling a handle from the pot.*

*by tapping with a fingertip. Score also with the toothbrush.*

*2 Bring the butt end up the pot and, supporting the wall inside the pot, press the two firmly together. Carefully weld the edges of the join.*

*3 Once you are satisfied it is securely fixed, hold up the pot with the handle hanging vertically down over a bowl of water and continue thinning and refining the handle just as described on page 61. Do not let the handle over-thin or weaken in any spot, particularly close to the pot. Keep the handle hanging vertically from the pot all the time.*

Place the palm of your pulling hand flat behind the handle with your fingertips touching the pot, and stand the pot on the edge of a clean surface, holding the handle (now horizontal).

*4 Now with the free hand, hold the end of the handle, and slide out the supporting hand, leaving a finger beneath the handle close to the pot. Allow the handle to drop over the finger into a natural curve and lightly adhere the end lower down the wall.*

*5 Study the handle's length, curve and line, adjusting its lower fixing up, down, to the right or to the left accordingly, before trimming and welding securely.*

*6 Stand the pot up to examine the hang of the handle. Subtle alterations to its curve may be carried out by stroking its inside surface with a wet finger. (A droop may be corrected by drying the pot standing on its rim.)*

*Wide-bellied jug by the author. Thrown in one piece, with handle pulled from the pot. Slip-decorated earthenware, 28 cm high.*

# HANDLE REFINEMENT

The physical and visual strength of a handle lies in secure foundations, even thickness and clean, natural curves. Weight, length and character should be dictated by the pot.

The illustrations below emphasize these points and offer some alternative ways to finish off a handle at the lower end.

(A) and (B) are examples of handles pulled from the pot. (C), (D) and (E) are parallel loops. The method of finish, at the lower end, may be carried out on either.

Note particularly that the area of fixing top and bottom is substantial. Each is welded quite firmly before cosmetic styling.

A 'Butterfly wings' created with a flourish by the flick of a thumb.
B Blended in seamlessly.
C The tail is folded upwards into a loop.
D The tail is rolled back into a scroll.
E A small coil is welded into the 'V' between handle and pot as either a visual or physical reinforcement (this is done once the handle has become leather-hard).

# ALTERNATIVE METHODS OF HANDLE-MAKING

The desire for purely ornamental decoration and embellishment can be combined with the practical need for a functional handle or knob by applying hand-modelled shapes, figurative or otherwise, by the use of textured slabs or coils, or with extrusions.

## COMBING OR SLEDGING
A profile may be cut into the straight edge of a sheet of stiff plastic or thin metal (such as a lid cut in half). Sponge the surface of a strip of soft clay and comb the profile along its length once or twice.

## EXTRUSIONS
An extruding machine consists of a barrel, a screw plunger and some metal die plates. The profile is cut out of the plate and the clay is forced through the aperture. A cheap and simple alternative is to make a wire loop and draw it through a block or coil of clay.

### Making a wire extruder
The wires that seal bags of clay are ideal for the purpose. Using pointed pliers, first straighten out the kinks, then bend the wire into shape, twisting the ends into a stem with which to grip. Coathanger wire is tougher to work, but suitable for larger extrusions.

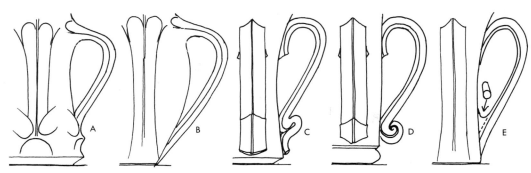

*Handle refinement.*

**Extruding the clay**

1 Prepare your clay well and form it into a fat coil or block wide enough to accommodate the loop. The clay *must* be soft.

2 Hold the stem vertically and draw it swiftly and steadily through the clay with the loop buried beneath the surface.

3 Carefully fold back the flaps and lift out the extrusion, keeping it straight and lying it good side up.

(A tall, narrow block of clay can be used to make a number of extrusions. Trim off the flaps with a wire before repeating.)

*Note* Extruded handles are inherently weaker than pulled ones and so must be used with care. Keep them moist (covered in plastic until ready to use) and *don't* flex them until they are shaped on the pot.

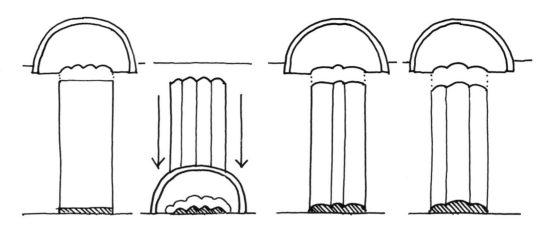

*(Above right) Sledged or combed straps.*

*(Right) Extruding handles with a wire loop.*

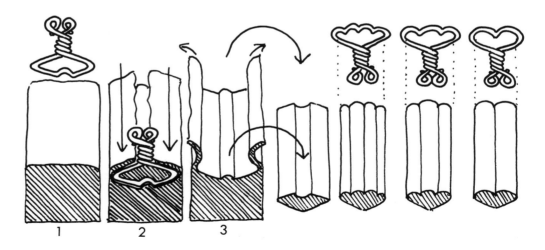

# CHAPTER SEVEN

# LIDS

## LIDDED FORMS

Making an open form into an enclosed container involves throwing a second, separate element to complete the piece. This lid or cover may be a simple saucer shape with a knob, it may have a function of its own as a cup, bowl or measuring scoop and/or it may form the larger element of the two pieces (for example, a bell cover to a shallow dish or plate).

The shape and size of lid and pot and the method by which the one sits on or in the other is dictated by both practical functions – cooking, serving or storing liquids or solids, hot or cold – and pure aesthetics.

Broadly speaking, to make the one sit securely on the other, you have two options – either the pot has to have a step or 'gallery' to hold a plain lid, or the lid has to have a device such as a flange to hold it onto a plain rim. The illustrations here are of some typical examples of both types.

**1 Gallery**
*Aperture of pot is narrowed, giving good heat retention.*

**2 Flange lid**
*Acts as a good dust cover and allows easy access to the pot with its plain edge.*
**3 Cap**
*Again a good dust cover. Lid may be used as a measuring or drinking cup.*

**4 Concave 'sunk-in' lid**
*Lid is thrown upright and finished in one go. Pot has a curved, slanting gallery.*
**5 Flanged 'drop-in' lid**
*Again thrown upright. Rim of pot is plain.*
**6 Flush gallery lid counter-weighted for a teapot*

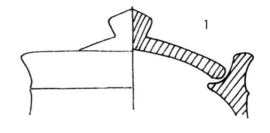
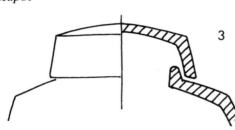
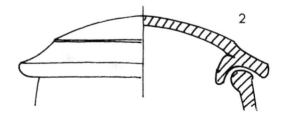
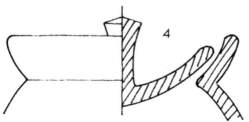

*Types of lid.*

*Flange-lidded jar by Phil Rogers. Ridges pressed out from inside and combed. Beech-ash glaze, oilfired stoneware, 38 cm high.*

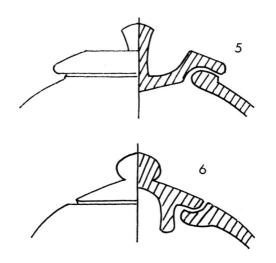

5

6

# FORMING A GALLERY

The method shown here is one of many ways in which potters achieve the same ends. The shape and finished quality of the gallery and the neck of the pot will vary according to scale, use and stylistic approach. The end result should be crisp and distinct, with the profile of the gallery nicely rounded for the rounded rim of the lid to sit comfortably. Provided your measurement is accurate, only a slight shelf is required. An unnecessarily wide one will only restrict access to the contents and be prone to chipping.

*1 The pot is only semi-thrown when the gallery-forming begins. (Applying downward pressure on the rim may cause a fully thinned wall to buckle.) Enough clay is left at the rim on which to work.*
*2 Just supporting with a light pinch beneath the rim, the index finger begins to form a right-angled groove.*
*3 The gallery is fully formed, taking care not to overthin its inside edge and preserving a substantial rim on the pot.*
*4 The pot is now thrown up to full height and any further bellying can take place.*
*5 The gallery is further refined with a table knife. This leaves a good, crisp, clean finish and its pressure is light enough not to distort the form. Take special care not to make the rim of the gallery curl in or overhang as this can cause the lid to be trapped during kiln firing. Chamois smooth.*

*6 Measuring*
*This is the all-important part of successful lidded-pot making. The finished lid needs to be neither too tight nor too loose. Expand your callipers to build in a slight tolerance. Set one tip to the rim's inside edge (the widest point on the aperture). Set the other tip just wider than the inside edge of the gallery (the narrowest point of the aperture). This should give you the small degree of play required.*

## MAKING THE LID

This is the simplest of shallow saucers (*note:* not a bowl with an upright rim) with a good rounded rim, of a weight that is in scale with the pot. Here a knob will be attached after it has been trimmed. Its gentle curve will carry on from the belly of the pot. Note how, having made an allowance with your callipers for a nice fit, the lid must be thrown *exactly* to the callipers' width.

*Measuring the lid.*

*Forming a gallery.*

Lidded jar by the author. Flanged lid with pulled handle. Slip-decorated earthenware.

## MAKING A FLANGED LID

This is more or less the reverse of the previous exercise. The gallery is on the lid instead of on the pot. The simple part of this is making the pot.

The pot rim has extra weight and width and is nicely rounded with a very slight overhang at the narrowest point of the neck. It is this point that you must measure with the callipers. Again, just as before, to make a nice fit a little leeway must be built into your measurement. Expand the callipers to within a few millimetres of the width. It is sensible to measure across in two or three positions around the circumference to make sure the pot is not badly distorted.

Calculating how much clay to use for the lid is a matter of experience. The overall width of this lid is wider than the pot and will need perhaps two or three times as much weight as the simple saucer shown on page 68 for a pot of similar width. (A wide, shallow dish may need the same weight for both the pot and the lid.)

1 *Throw a saucer with a thick rim, with an overall width a little more than your callipers.*
2 *Thin this rim into a wall, sloping inwards at about a 45° angle.*
3 *Now, holding up the rim of that wall, fold in the wall with a fingertip. Check progress with the callipers.*
4 *Slow the wheel and pinch out the rim, taking care not to flatten the flange. Measure with the callipers again.*

5 *Use a table knife to refine the gallery (try to mirror the curve of the pot rim). Chamois smooth.*
6 **Measuring**
*Note which width the callipers measure. It is the* outside *edge of the flange (it must be a precise measurement – remember, the allowance for play has already been taken into account). The cut-away section shows how the width of clay is wide enough to support the overhanging rim.*

Measuring the pot.

*Making a flanged lid.*

# MAKING KNOBS AND HANDLES FOR LIDS

You may leave enough thickness on the base of your lid from which to turn a knob, exactly as you would turn a footring. Alternatively the lid can be trimmed into a smooth, shallow dome to which a knob or another type of handle may be applied.

## APPLYING AND THROWING A KNOB

*1 Centre and fix down the turned lid securely. Check that the lid is not too thin at the centre. Roll a ball of plastic clay and flatten on one side. Score flattened surface and centre of lid-well. Apply a little slurry.*
*2 Centre and stick down the knob.*
*3 Weld the seam into the lid.*
*4 Once firmly in place, using as little water as you can, throw and refine.*

If the lid and knob are quite large, it is helpful to pre-throw the knob shape on the wheel.

*Throwing a knob on a lid.*

*Applying a strap handle to a lid.*

## APPLYING A STRAP HANDLE

Use a parallel strap which has a scale and quality that suit the lid and pot. Assess the length you will need and trim the ends of the strap accordingly.

*1 Roughen the joining areas on the lid with a wet toothbrush. Apply a little slurry if the strap is already fairly stiff.*
*2 Holding the strap at either end, allow it to drop into a suitable curve (good side facing down). Flip it over and place it on the lid. Adjust its position and height and ensure that it straddles the very centre of the dome.*
*3 Pick up the lid support behind the join as you weld the ends securely in place.*
*4 If necessary, use a wet finger on the underside of the handle to adjust its position and refine its curve.*

### SIDE HANDLES OR LUGS ON A POT WALL

Pull a strap long enough to make two handles. Follow steps (1) and (2) above, but when flipped over, twist the ends of the strap to face you. Stick the ends in place, adjust and weld.

# CHAPTER EIGHT

# TEAPOTS

The teapot embodies the true test of the thrower's skill and artistry. A form has to be made from three separately thrown elements which, when put together, must be lightweight to handle, perform a very specialized function and hang together visually as a complete object.

## THE BODY
For the leaves to be infused into the hot liquid, the form needs to be squat, and to retain its heat, narrow-necked. Whether round-bellied, cylindrical or conical, the walls must be thin, even and smooth enough to weld on the spout cleanly.

## THE LID
The lid can be made in a wide variety of fittings, but must fit accurately, be lightweight and have a low centre of gravity – that is, bottom- rather than top-heavy, so that it stays in place when the teapot is tipped at a steep angle. Devices can be used to make the lid stay in place, but will restrict you in your

design. A small hole piercing the lid improves pouring by breaking the vacuum created. The knob must be easy to hold and tall enough not to become hot to the touch.

## THE SPOUT
The spout is a tapering cone or funnel with a wide diameter at the join and a narrow neck to compress and direct the water flow. The

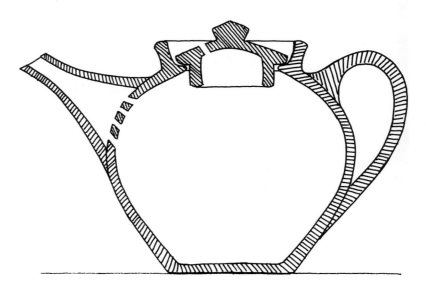

*The elements of a teapot.*

*Porcelain teapot and mugs by Derek Emms. Carved decoration, blue celadon glaze. Photo courtesy of* Ceramic Review.

mouth of the spout should be level with or just higher than the filling level of the body, and should be cut cleanly and crisply at an angle that will discourage dribbling.

## THE HANDLE

A side handle should above all appear to balance out the angle, weight and length of the spout. A cane handle (over the top) must be tall enough to allow access to the lid.

# THROWING OFF THE HUMP

It is not always necessary or convenient to weigh out individual pieces of clay for throwing. Smaller items can be made and cut from a cone or hump of clay. You assess approximately how much clay you will need to make a particular pot, and physically divide off that amount with a waistline. After making and removing each piece, the lump is re-centred and divided off again, allowing you to make several pieces of perhaps different sizes or widths. Small bowls, lids and teapot spouts are very suitable candidates for this method. See opposite for illustrations.

*1 Begin as if you were centring a large piece of clay, but do not use more than you can easily handle. Cone up the lump into a wide-based cone (not too tall and slender). Concentrate on centring just the small waisted top.*
*2 The lid illustrated here is made all in one,*

*Teapot by Takeshi Yasuda. Over-the-top handle, sprigged decoration, three-colour glaze, oxidized stoneware. Photo Takeshi Yasuda.*

*Throwing a sunk-in lid 'off the hump'.*

*with little or no need for trimming. It takes the form of a saucer with a knob in the centre. The first move is to divide the knob from the saucer.*

**3** *The width is pulled out and measured and the knob is refined chamois-smooth.*

**4** *The completed lid is then divided off from the lump with a crisp V-shaped cut. Do not take with it more weight than you need.*

**5** *To cut off horizontally, loop a length of strong thread around the clay (in the direction of wheel rotation) right into the groove of the V. Now turn the wheel very slowly, whilst keeping a grip on the end of the thread. The thread tightens into a knot and in one revolution will cut the lid free.*

**6** *Lift off with forked fingers.*

## THROWING A SPOUT

Judging how much clay to use takes some practice. The method shown opposite creates a spout with its own base from which it is later cut, so make your calculation to allow for this waste. A long-necked, wide-based spout can always be cut down to size, but a short, narrow one will be of no use if it is out of scale with the body.

*1 Centre a wide, flattish dome, hollow down with a single finger and undercut right out to the width of the centred clay. With the fingertips only, pull up into a tall, tapering cone with a concave profile. Do not overthin.*

*Teapot by Walter Keeler. Body thrown upside-down, creased and cut before being applied to a slab base. Creased spout and extruded handle. Salt-glazed stoneware, 20 cm high.*

*Throwing a spout.*

**2** *Using thumbs and first two fingers, collar the cone into a deeper, concave curve with a narrower neck. If the form is already overthinned, it will buckle.*
**3** *Now that the spout is too narrow for a finger, use a smooth, round stick to thin and raise the spout further, throwing against it with the fingertips. Be careful to use enough lubrication or the spout will twist and buckle.*
**4** *Finally, use a rib or kidney to refine the curve and surface. Make a bevel below the spout and cut off with its solid base.*

## APPLYING A SPOUT

This may be done with a soft or leather-hard spout. Leather-hard spouts have to be carefully cut and carved to fit onto the pot. Applying them when soft, although a little trickier to handle, allows you to mould the spout seamlessly onto the body. It is the second method that is shown here (see overleaf). The teapot body and its lid should be ready-trimmed, refined and leather-hard. Put the lid to one side.

**1** *For the spout to rise from the body at an upward angle, it must be cut from its base at a suitable slant. A sawing action will prevent it collapsing as the wire is pulled through.*
**2** *With a dry hand, lightly grip the spout and lift it up to the pot. Touch it on, approximately where it will join, making sure the mouth comes at least level with the rim of the body. The faint wet rim left on the body will*

*Applying a spout.*

*mark your area for drilling the straining holes. Replace the spout temporarily on its base.*

*3 With a hole borer (4–5 mm) cut plenty of holes in a regular pattern (this improves the pouring flow). With a wet toothbrush, score thoroughly in a broad ring around the holes.*

*4 Pick up the spout again and with a wet fingertip gently flare the joining edge. Lightly score with the toothbrush, stroking outwards across the edge.*

*5 Offer up the spout to the body and lightly touch it on. Pick up the body and adjust the spout position for height and alignment over the straining holes before carefully blending in the flared edge. Begin with the sides and top, then work around the underside, taking care not to crease the throat.*

*6 As the spout hardens, further blending and smoothing can be carried out with a metal kidney. Trim the length and angle of the spout mouth only when it has dried to leather-hard.*

## HANDLES

Always apply the handle last so that it may be balanced and aligned with the spout. This may be done as soon as the spout is on. To mimic the upward thrust of the spout, it may help to stand the pot on its rim and allow the handle to dry hanging at a similar angle.

*Teapot by the author. Flanged lid, handles pulled from the body and lid. Slip-decorated earthenware, 20 cm high.*

# CHAPTER NINE

# CHARACTER, PERSONALITY AND DESIGN

## RIMS

Whilst your energies are concentrated on the techniques of throwing, the aesthetics of the vessel are more difficult to address. Your awareness of the importance of form, shape and style only heightens your frustration until your level of skill begins to match your ambition to make visually pleasing and well-balanced pots.

One of the cornerstones of the aesthetic and functional strength of thrown pottery is the rim. It is a focal point which, if neglected, so often lets down a good, attractively proportioned form.

With subtle weight distribution, an elegant and delicate character can be underpinned with a disguised sturdiness in the neck. Conversely, an appearance of weight can be created with concealed hollows and undercuts.

Blurred and slurry-coated rim walls are enhanced by using a rib to clean and reveal the crisp texture of the clay, and to create creases, curves or facets.

## FOOTRINGS

They may not share the rim's conspicuous position, but the quality of a footring is of equal importance to the form it supports. Turning a pot over to study the bottom is a well-known potter's habit. Assessing a vessel from every aspect becomes second nature.

Whether a tall, shapely stem, a roughly hewn collar or a clean continuation of the wall's silhouette, the footring's weight and width must reflect the function and character of the form as a whole.

A tapered stem can lighten the appearance of a pot considerably. A slight flare is practical to hold when glazing. Curving the underside of the footring prevents chipping, and by reducing its surface contact with a kiln shelf, helps to prevent sticking.

## SURFACES

An undecorated surface is by no means featureless. The characteristic spiral lines and grooves known as 'throwing rings' are a natural result of the process. They will vary according to pressure and speed, but if created self-consciously will appear contrived.

Grog, sand or other 'fillers' will be exposed by scouring the rotating surfaces with a metal kidney or turning tool, or smoothed over by the action of a rib.

A natural combination of these effects, coated evenly with a good glaze, especially one that breaks in colour or quality over peaks and troughs, will pick out the lightest of textural variation and nuances of hand on clay. Over-fastidious use of sponge or finger during leather-hard finishing so often wipes away these major contributors to a vessel's life and spontaneity.

## SETS AND RANGES

To be able to make a matching set of something is always one of the elusive goals of throwing students. Undoubtedly the basic techniques have to be practised many times before your results begin to approach a satisfying similarity. It is not simply a matter

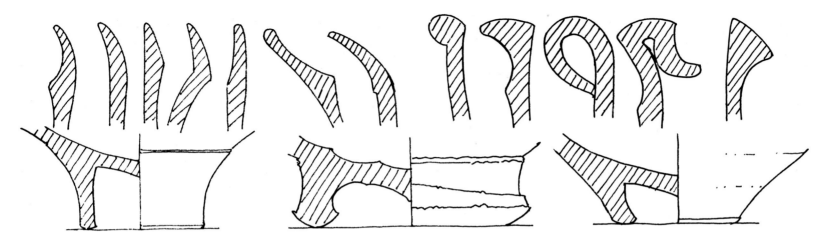

*Rims and footrings.*

of weights and measures. Although they are important, it is the subtle touch of hand and tool that gives your pots the personality and character that really count. The quality of a curve, a rim, a footring or a handle, a banded line or a simple decoration are all elements which may unify a group to make a set. A set can become a range when the unifying features are successfully transferred to other vessels giving them a family resemblance.

## TO MAKE A SHRINKAGE RULER
Lay a blank stick alongside a ruler and mark off the key figures arrowed with an indelible pen or scored line. Continue to subdivide the 'shrinkage centimetres' with similar marks.

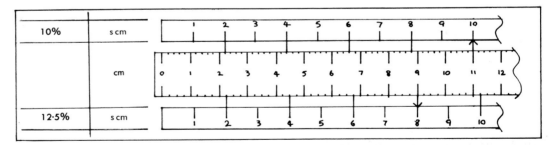

*How to make a shrinkage ruler.*

*Repetition throwing (see opposite for instructions).*

# WEIGHTS AND MEASURES

Listed here are some typical items of domestic pottery and suggested weights of clay to make them. The volumes and dimensions given represent fired and finished sizes. Using a shrinkage ruler will compensate for the overall reduction in size of your pots from wet to glaze-fired. The widths given are in 'shrinkage centimetres' (s cm).

| Item | Approx. minimum size | Clay weight (grams) |
|---|---|---|
| **Flat-based forms** | | |
| Mug | 200 ml | 280 |
| Jug | 225 ml | 350 |
| Jug | 500 ml | 500 |
| Jug | 1 l | 1000 |
| Jug | 2 l | 1800 |
| Side plate | 17 s cm wide | 570 |
| Dinner plate | 25 s cm wide | 1100 |
| Teapot | 4-cup | 680 |
| Teapot | 6-cup | 1100 |
| Casserole dish | 1 l | 1150 |
| Casserole dish | 2 l | 1900 |
| Casserole dish | 3 l | 2250 |
| Storage jar | 500 ml | 520 |
| Storage jar | 1 l | 1050 |
| Storage jar | 2 l | 1850 |
| **Curved-base forms (turning required)** | | |
| Cup | 10 s cm wide | 350 |
| Saucer | 17 s cm wide | 650 |
| Bowl | 15 s cm wide | 550 |
| Bowl | 25 s cm wide | 1500 |
| Bowl | 30 s cm wide | 2500 |
| Dish or plate | 25 s cm wide | 1400 |
| Wide-rimmed platter | 30 s cm wide | 2250 |
| Wide-rimmed platter | 40 s cm wide | 4750 |
| Casserole lids (30–100% of pot weight) | | |
| Storage-jar lids (20–65% of pot weight) | | |

*Note*   Plain, narrow lids need least; flanged, wide lids need most.

# REPETITION THROWING

For this you will need an adjustable measuring pointer, a device fixed firmly either to the wheel or to a bracket alongside it, which can be set level with the height and width of the pot rim. The best type has a hinged tip which will swing out of the way whilst you centre the clay. A double pointer can measure a pot in two places (for example at the belly width as well as the rim).

**METHOD** (*see illustrations opposite*)
Throw several pots until you are happy that you have created the form you want, with a good height, width and volume for its weight (cut through the trial pots to check if there are any glaringly thick areas).

*1 Set the pointer to within 2 or 3 mm of the rim, then swing away the tip and cut and lift off the pot.*
*2 Centre and hollow out the next piece of clay.*
*3 Pull up the primary wall before resetting the pointer.*
*4 Throw on the pot until approximate height and width are reached.*
*5 Carry out the subtle adjustments to the form and other usual refinements.*
*6 Accuracy will improve in time, but the pure measurement is subordinate to the quality of the pot. You need to settle into a rhythm, repeating your procedure of pulling up, ribbing and refining each time until the routine becomes automatic. The more repeats*

*Woodfired stoneware by John Leach. The small casserole has a thrown pan handle. Photo Rob Pedersen.*

*you do the more your technique will gel and the more the forms will unify. At the end of the batch, make notes about the weight, dimensions and form (annotating points on your original design if you wish) so that you have it to refer to another time.*

# SURFACE DECORATION ON THE WET CLAY

The rotation of the potter's wheel provides you with the means to band, comb and profile the clay with simple but effective designs of linear symmetry, one of the particular trade marks of throwing. Decorating tools can be bought or made from a variety of metals, fine-grained timbers like boxwood or bamboo, or stiff plastics. Devise your own with odds and ends of machinery, DIY tools or kitchen implements. Where crisp lines are desired, tools with V-shaped teeth are more effective because they do not leave a burred edge.

Just as any artist wants a clean slate or blank sheet to work on, a smooth, ribbed surface offers the potter a fresh canvas.

Hold the tool as you would a rib, at right-angles to the surface or sloping slightly so that the blade points in the direction of the revolving wall. Experiment with various speeds of rotation and oscillations of the tool to create wave patterns.

*Surface decoration on plastic clay.*

*Tableware by Andrew and Joanna Young. Rouletted and pressed decoration. Stoneware. Photo Oliver Riviere.*

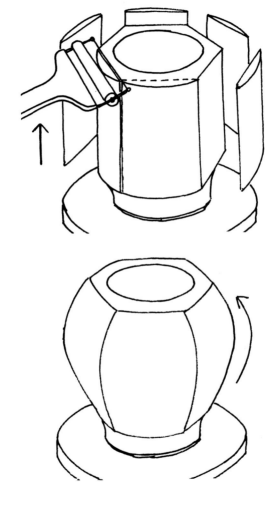

*Cutting facets.*

# ALTERING THE FORM IN THE PLASTIC STATE

## DISTORTION

Whilst the pot is very plastic, the round form can be distorted by creasing the walls and/or the rim. Divide off the circumference into sections. With fingers, stretch the rim at opposite sides and with fingers or tool score or crease up the wall.

Rims may be pinched, folded or stretched (perhaps in a similar method to jug-lip making).

## CUTTING FACETS

Walls may be thrown intentionally thick and sliced vertically into rough facets, and perhaps further bellied (see left).

# SURFACE DECORATION ON THE LEATHER-HARD CLAY

Once a vessel is leather-hard, it may be crisply carved, scratched or combed either through a slip coating as a contrast to the clay colour, or onto the plain surface. Using a wheel or other hard, textured implements, patterns may be rolled or pressed. Textured clay may be adhered to the pot surface to create low relief. All these types of decoration can be highlighted by a glazing effect.

### Piercing
Perforating the pot wall with patterns of window shapes.

### Fluting
Vertical grooves are cut into the pot wall around the circumference. Using a special tool or simply a broad, square-ended blade, hold the pot surface horizontally and make the cuts in swift, firm strokes. The pot wall must be flat or only slightly bellied and it helps to have a distinct starting line, such as an angled edge.

### Sprigging
Textured features, motifs or symbols are cast in small, one-piece plaster moulds, or carved into biscuit-fired clay stamps. Repeats of the press-moulded or stamped shapes may be arranged in patterns on the pot surface.

### Altering the form in the leather-hard state
Forms may be distorted by pressing with the hands or by beating or patting with rigid implements (textured or plain) of wood or metal to create creases or facets.
*Note* Cracking or splitting will occur if the pot is too hard.

## MAKING DISTORTED DISHES

1 Throw a baseless vertical wall on a bat.
2 When stiff but not too hard, wire through and press into the desired shape.
3 Allow to stiffen further, then turn onto the rim to score and slurry the bottom of the wall.
4 Roll out a slab base.
5 Turn the prepared wall onto the slab.
6 Press firmly in place, trim up the slab and finish the join inside and out.

*Faceted bottle by Mike Dodd. Granite glaze coated in local iron and over-dipped with a tenmoku glaze. Oil/woodfired stoneware, 23 cm high.*

*Distorted dish by Jane Hamlyn. Modelled handles on a textured slab base. Salt-glazed stoneware.*

# CUTTING AND RE-ASSEMBLING

When you are no longer limited in your basic throwing techniques, the potter's wheel can be used to create elements of more complex, sculptural forms. Cylindrical sections, while retaining the character of a wheel-thrown form and surface, can be cut up and distorted in the leather-hard state, then re-assembled into stylized versions of familiar vessels or quite abstract constructions altogether. Manipulation of the material requires skill and precision to produce finished objects which combine technical or aesthetic strength. Weak or uneven throwing will be intolerant of this distortion and reconstruction. Potters often develop their own clay bodies to cope with the demands of their advanced techniques and creative ideas.

*(Left) Articulated jug by Walter Keeler. Extruded handle. Salt-glazed stoneware.*

*(Right) Thrown slab piece, five elements, by Colin Pearson. Oxidized stoneware, 31 cm high. Photo Colin Pearson.*

*Three jugs by Clive Bowen. Slip-decorated, woodfired earthenware. Photo David Cripps.*

# BIBLIOGRAPHY

## TECHNIQUES AND PHILOSOPHY

Casson, Michael *The Craft of the Potter* (BBC Publications, 1991)

Colbeck, John *Pottery: The Technique of Throwing* (Batsford, 1991)

Leach, Bernard *A Potter's Book* (Faber & Faber, 1991)

Rhodes, Daniel *Pottery Form* (Pitman Publishing; now out of print but available from libraries or second-hand bookshops)

## VESSEL FORM: SOURCES OF INSPIRATION

### ANCIENT

Museum collections and publications on Greek, Roman, Islamic, African, Chinese, Japanese, Korean and Medieval European pottery.

### TWENTIETH CENTURY

Birks, Tony *Hans Coper* (Marston House, 1983)

Birks, Tony *Lucie Rie* (Alphabooks/A & C Black, 1987)

Clark, Garth *Michael Cardew* (Faber & Faber, 1978; now out of print but available from libraries or second-hand bookshops)

*Bernard Leach, Hamada and their Circle* (Phaidon/Christie's, 1990)

## SPECIALIST MAGAZINES

For features and information on potters, pottery courses and suppliers:

*Ceramic Review*
21 Carnaby Street
London W1V IPH

*Ceramics Monthly*
Professional Publications Inc.
Box 12448
Columbus
Ohio 43212
USA

# INDEX